RAILWAY HISTORY IN PICTURES:
WALES AND THE WELSH BORDER COUNTIES

The 'Cambrian Coast Express' through train between Paddington and Aberystwyth, near Talerddig in 1963, hauled by Great Western 4–6–0 No 7819 **Hinton Manor**

RAILWAY HISTORY IN PICTURES

Wales and the Welsh
Border Counties

H. C. CASSERLEY

DAVID & CHARLES : NEWTON ABBOT

ISBN 0 7153 4975 9

Set in 10 on 12 pt Plantin
and printed in Great Britain
by W. J. Holman Limited Dawlish
for David & Charles (Publishers) Limited
South Devon House Newton Abbot Devon

CONTENTS

MAPS pages 10 and 108

INTRODUCTION

The ancient Principality of Wales can provide more than its full share of fascinating railway history, notwithstanding that railroad development lagged somewhat behind most other parts of the country. Although the north-east of England, with its associations with George Stephenson and other pioneer railway engineers, must rightly be regarded on a general basis as the birthplace of railways throughout the world, nevertheless Wales can claim absolute priority in at least two respects, and, in a more modern context, in a third.

It saw the first steam locomotive ever to run on rails; it had the first public passenger carrying railway in the world, and in more recent times it pioneered the birth of the modern preservation movement, which has taken place entirely during the last twenty years.

Taken as a whole, Wales undoubtedly offers by far the widest range of variety in interest in the railway world to be found in any comparable area of the United Kingdom, ranging from scenic lines of superb beauty to the utilitarian industrial field.

Essentially the home of the narrow gauge, a number of which systems still survive, mostly through the efforts of preservation societies, these too possess a charm and attraction hardly to be compared elsewhere.

It is interesting also to note that it can claim the highest rail altitudes attained in the British Isles, on both narrow and standard gauges, the 1,484 ft at Druimuachdar on the Highland Railway in Scotland, well known as the highest main line passenger railway, being in fact exceeded by a good margin on an industrial line in South Wales.

Within the limited scope of this volume, which cannot pretend to cover more than the very briefest sketches of actual historical record, will be found a wide selection of illustrations, old and new, covering many aspects of the railway history of this unique country.

EARLY DEVELOPMENT

The Principality of Wales covers an area of 7,446 square miles, divided amongst twelve counties, not counting Monmouthshire. Mostly it is a hill country, from the mountainous Snowdonia region in the north, the Cambrian Mountains in central Wales, to the Brecon Beacons and coal valleys in the south, flanked only by a few comparatively flat areas of the south coastal plain bordering the Bristol Channel, and the Isle of Anglesey in the north-west, separated from the mainland by the Menai Straits.

Over the whole country, one half of the land reaches an altitude of 600 ft above sea level, whilst one half of this again exceeds some 1,000 ft and there are a good many areas over 2,000 ft high.

At the beginning of the nineteenth century Wales and Monmouthshire had a population of something over half a million, fairly evenly distributed, as it was concerned mainly with agriculture. The Industrial Revolution of the 1840s changed all this, as the growth of industry led to a large concentration of population in the rich coal and iron producing area of south-east Wales, and by the 1920s more than half the population of the entire area was concentrated in the two counties of Glamorgan and Monmouth. The last mentioned, although technically outside the principality, is usually regarded for practical purposes as part of Wales. This is the main reason why the scope of this book has been widened to include the 'border counties', part of which fit naturally into the concept of Wales as a whole.

Generally speaking, railway development did not get off to quite such an early start as in some other parts of the country, notably the north-east, rightly regarded as the birthplace of railways in the true sense, which took place in the early part of the nineteenth century. There had of course been primitive tramroads or plateways, for the conveyance of coal and other minerals, long before that in many parts of the country, although they do not seem to have appeared in South Wales much before about 1790.

Nevertheless, Wales can claim priority in railway history in two very important respects: firstly, it saw the first ever steam locomotive to run on rails, built by Richard Trevithick in 1804, and which ran on the Pen-y-Darren Tramroad, Merthyr Tydfil (opened in 1800). As such it antedated by a good many years Hedley's **Wylam Dilly** of 1812, the oldest locomotive still in existence, and of course the very much better known early locomotives such as George Stephenson's **Locomotion** and **Rocket** of later years.

Trevithick's 1804 engine, the first steam locomotive to run on rails.

The other respect in which Wales can claim to have partaken in railway history lies in the fact that it saw the first public passenger railway in the world, authorised by Parliament on 29 June 1804 in the reign of King George III. This, the Oystermouth Railway at Swansea, conveyed its first passengers on 25 March 1807, of course with horse traction, as a number of years were yet to pass before rail transport with steam locomotives became a practical possibility. It was not until 1877 that steam engines were introduced on the Oystermouth Railway, at first of the enclosed type, then coming into general use as local roadside lines, but in 1892 0–6–0STs of conventional design made their appearance. In the meantime it became known as the Swansea & Mumbles Railway Co Ltd, to be taken over in 1899 by the Swansea Improvements & Tramway Company, the lease being transferred in 1927 to the South Wales Transport Company Ltd.

In 1929 it was electrified, and henceforth operated by tramcars of conventional design, extremely large vehicles, and probably the biggest of their kind in the country. In this form it continued until, on 4 January 1960, it succumbed finally to bus competition, although it carried a heavy traffic to the end.

As has already been mentioned, it was the first public passenger railway to be authorised by Parliament, although it was antedated by four others which were built for the conveyance of goods only, the earliest being the Surrey Iron Railway in 1801, followed by two others, the Carmarthenshire and the Sirhowy, with the Croydon, Godstone & Merstham in 1803. Of these, all but the Sirhowy had long since been abandoned, and the last mentioned lost its original identity when it became part of the LNWR branch through Tredegar to Newport. At the time of closure the Swansea & Mumbles was therefore rightly described as the 'Oldest Railway in the World'. The Carmarthenshire Railway, a tramroad company, was incorporated in 1802, and authorised to construct a 16-mile line from Llanelly Flats to Castell-y-Garreg lime works, near the present Llandebi station, and was opened in two stages in 1803-4. Although the use of locomotives was authorised in 1834, this was never implemented, and the line gradually fell into disuse.

There had been earlier tramroads authorised by Parliament during the latter half of the eighteenth

Horse-drawn train on the Oystermouth Railway about 1855. Other pictures of this line, eventually known as the Swansea & Mumbles Tramway, will be found on page 82.

century, the oldest of all being the Brandling line of of 1758, which still survives as the Middleton Railway, Leeds. This was followed by seventeen others before the inception of the Surrey Iron Railway in 1801, but none of them were public lines, with the possible exception of the Middleton itself, concerning which some doubt exists.

As already mentioned, railway development in Wales as a whole was comparatively slow compared with the rest of the country. In 1844, for instance, the beginning of the period known as the Railway Mania, only two short conventional railways were in operation, the Taff Vale, between Merthyr and Cardiff, with one or two branches, some 25 miles in all, and the Llanelly Railway, from Llanelly to Brynamman, with branches, a total of 28 route miles.

The South Wales Railway (later part of the GWR), extending right through from Monmouth to the west coast, was authorised, but not yet built, whilst in the north the Chester and Holyhead, planned as part of the main through route to Ireland, which it did in fact become, was likewise under construction, but not actually completed throughout until 1850.

By 1852 more lines had appeared in the South Wales coalfield, and much of the projected through route between Chester, Shrewsbury, Hereford and Newport, was in operation, but the entire central area of Wales west of this line, including the whole of the shores of Cardigan Bay, was still without railways, although England itself was, by this time, served by a comprehensive network of lines. It was in the following year, 1853, however, that the first beginnings of what was to become the Cambrian Railways, which later did much to fill the gap, were seen in the authorisation of the small Llanidloes & Newtown Railway, eventually opened in 1859, followed by the Oswestry and Newtown, authorised in 1855 and opened in 1860. Machynlleth was reached in 1863, and eventually Aberystwyth in 1864, the west coast at last being reached, followed by other extensions which gave the coast of Cardigan Bay its much needed rail facilities.

The central part of Wales, with its sparse population, has never been attractive to the rail promoter, and had the Beeching proposals been implemented to the full it seems likely that the position would almost have reverted to 1852, leaving a vast area devoid of rail facilities, although at the time of writing the through route is still open to Aberystwyth and the central Wales line from Craven Arms down through Llandovery manages to maintain a precarious existence, although under constant threat of closure.

Such then is a very general overall, if necessarily very brief, outline of the earlier history of the development of railways in Wales. It will not of course be possible to go into subsequent history in any great detail in such a small volume, but short summaries, supplemented by suitable illustrations, taking each area or feature in turn, should help to provide a general picture of the railways as a whole.

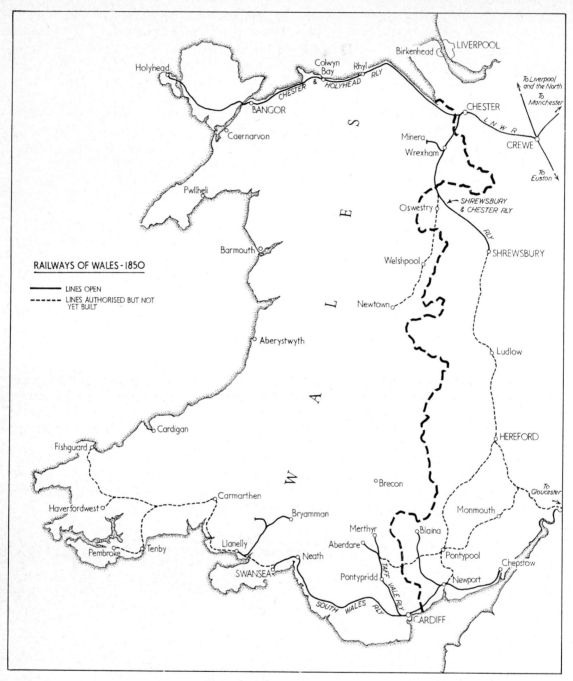

RAILWAYS OF WALES - 1850

LINES OPEN
LINES AUTHORISED BUT NOT
YET BUILT

Must it come back to this?

Had the Beeching proposals of 1964 been implemented to the full, the railway map of Wales would have reverted to something like this. Fortunately saner and more realistic appreciation of the social and economic needs of the country prevailed.

THE CHESTER & HOLYHEAD RAILWAY

The first important main line in Wales was the Chester & Holyhead, incorporated in 1844. It was opened in sections between 1848 and 1850, in which year it was completed throughout, the last link being the Britannia Bridge crossing the Menai Straits to the Isle of Anglesey. The engineer was Robert Stephenson. The completion of the line reduced the time from London to Holyhead to 9 hours 35 minutes by the 'Irish Mail', incidentally the oldest named train in the world.

There were numerous branches, some of them built by independent companies, and others by the LNWR after it had absorbed the Chester & Holyhead, but all eventually became part of the LNWR system.

An early print of the Britannia Bridge. It is practically unchanged in general appearance today, although the expressions on the lions' faces now look, perhaps naturally, somewhat older and more mature! Possibly also a little bored after having witnessed a countless procession of tens of thousands of trains in the course of some 120 years. It will be noted that the train is travelling 'wrong line'. This must be attributed to artist's licence, there being no evidence that right-hand running was ever adopted*.

* Since this was written, the disastrous fire which occurred on 23 May 1970 has put the bridge out of action. At the time of going to press it appears that it may be several months before repairs can be completed, and then probably only on a single line. Meanwhile the ships have been diverted to Heysham.

BRITANNIA BRIDGE

ANGLESEY ENTRANCE.

For the construction of Holyhead Breakwater a 7 ft-gauge railway was built from a quarry on Holyhead Mountain. This was kept in operation for maintenance purposes for many years afterwards. The engine **Prince Albert**, illustrated, was the last survivor of four built by R. B. Longridge & Company, of Bedlington, Northumberland, in 1852. It worked until 1913 (when the line was converted to standard gauge, twenty years after the passing of the Great Western broad gauge), and lay derelict at the quarries for a long time afterwards, being in fact not finally broken up until about 1945.

The up 'Irish Mail' at the Admiralty Pier, Holyhead, about fifty years ago.

The decorative arch in the town wall at Conway, where the line skirts the base of Conway Castle. This view, taken in pregrouping days, shows a LNWR 'Cauliflower' 0–6–0.

Up 'Welshman' leaving Colwyn Bay about 1930. The engine is one of the 'Claughton' class, No 5968 **John o' Groats**.

Invitation card to the opening of New Holyhead Harbour in 1880.

THE LONDON & NORTH WESTERN
AND THE MIDLAND

London & North Western of course included the original Chester & Holyhead, already dealt with in the previous section, but the self-styled 'Premier Line' also possessed a number of other lines in the Principality. These included the Central Wales, evolved from several one-time independent concerns, together with incursions into what eventually became predominantly Great Western territory, extending as far as Swansea and Carmarthen, not to mention Newport, which was reached by virtue of running powers over the GWR from Nine Mile Point.

The Midland, that ambitious railway which managed to extend its spheres of operation, either by means of its own lines, jointly owned lines, or running powers, to almost every quarter of the kingdom, also secured its small stake in South Wales, having its own lines into Swansea, although divorced from its own system and access being by virtue of running powers over other railways.

The picturesque Blaenau Festiniog branch started life as the Conway & Llanrwst Railway in 1863, but was not completed throughout until 1881 by the LNWR, by which it had meantime been absorbed. The terminus at Blaenau Festiniog was also served by the GWR branch from Bala Junction, and the narrow-gauge Festiniog, both referred to later. This view, taken in 1961, gives a good idea of the scenic nature of the line. It shows a train conveying the transformer referred to on the next page, the engine being an LMS goods class 4.

The Festiniog branch abounds with numerous curves and tunnels, one of which, shown here, is the eighth longest in the country, 2 miles 333 yd. The view, taken in 1961, shows the passage of an out-of-gauge load over the single line, a transformer for the atomic power station at Trawsfynydd, on the GWR branch, now connected to the LNWR at Blaenau Festiniog to enable trainloads of atomic waste to be conveyed for disposal. It would hardly be practical or safe to transport such dangerous material by any other means, as a result of which one complete branch (and the stub end of another) which otherwise might by now have been entirely closed, has attained a considerable importance even in this modern age.

The Central Wales line passes through the barren and sparsely populated areas of Radnorshire and bordering counties, and is nowadays the only direct rail link through the country connecting the sharply divided areas of the north and south. This view shows the lonely signal box and platform at Sugar Loaf Summit, one of the most isolated parts of the route.

Amongst the railways of Wales were some of the highest summits to be found in the British Isles. Leaving aside the Snowdon Mountain rack railway, and certain narrow-gauge slate quarry systems, referred to later in this book, the fourth highest passenger standard-gauge line was located at Waenavon, 1,400 ft above sea level, on the LNWR branch from Brynmawr to Blaenavon, and this view, taken in 1958, shows the summit signal box after all traffic had ceased and the line was being used for the storage of wagons. This was not however the highest standard-gauge line in Wales, this distinction being held by the 1,600 ft Ebbw Vale quarry line (see page 91), which was also the ultimate height reached by any standard-gauge line in the United Kingdom.

Skirting the northern extremities of the South Wales coal valleys, the LNWR had its own line from Abergavenny Junction through to Merthyr (the final section being jointly owned with the Brecon & Merthyr Railway). This was a very steeply graded railway and was worked to a large extent by eight coupled tender and tank locomotives, assisted by the doughty little Webb 4 ft 3 in 0–6–2Ts, which performed wonders, in view of their diminutive size, over this difficult road. This historic view shows the last train to run over the line, a special organised by the Stephenson Locomotive Society, at Brynmawr on 5 January 1958, with engines 58926 (now preserved in Penrhyn Castle Museum, Bangor) and 49121.

(Opposite above) LNWR Brynmawr–Barry excursion train at Pontllanfraith on 14 July 1957 with G2 class 0–8–0 No 49409.

The Midland's penetration into Wales consisted of a line from Hereford to Brecon (access to Hereford being over the GWR via Worcester) which it reached after joining the Cambrian at Three Cocks Junction (see page 49). Beyond Brecon it possessed running powers over the Neath & Brecon to Ynis-y-Geinon, there regaining its own metals, southwards to Swansea, where it had its terminus at St Thomas, and north-wards to Brynamman, where it met the GWR. This view shows a pull-and-push train about to leave Brynamman for Swansea in 1948.

The MR approach into Swansea. A Johnson 0–6–0T running light in 1938 to the shed at Upper Bank. Further reference to the Midland Railway in this area will be found on page 60.

It had been the practice of the former LNWR to allocate an old engine, usually a 2–4–0 of the 'Samson' or 'Waterloo' class, to the principal depots in the country for departmental duties, such as running officers' saloons or on permanent way work. The one covering the North Wales area was located at Bangor and carried plates reading Engineer Bangor, in place of the former name and number plates. For similar duties in South Wales a Midland Railway Johnson 2–4–0 No 155 was sent to Abergavenny in 1933 and for a short time carried similar appropriate plates on the splashers, as shown in this rare photograph (opposite below). These plates were removed after a short time and the engine received the ordinary running number 20155 on the duplicate list. It remained at Abergavenny until 1946 when it was transferred to Nottingham, being scrapped in 1950.

An interesting aerial view of Swansea South Dock. In the bottom left-hand corner is the LNWR Victoria terminus, whilst upper left, just beyond the river bridge, is the MR St Thomas station. The main GWR is out of sight on the left, but directly opposite, on the far side of the river, are the East Dock lines and the Swansea Harbour Trust line (see page 70), whilst the site of the old Rhondda & Swansea Bay terminus was just short of the bridge.

EARLY CONSTITUENTS OF THE GWR IN SOUTH WALES

The earliest, and what was to become the principal, through trunk line in the southern half of the Principality, was the South Wales Railway, authorised in 1845, and planned to connect with the Great Western near Gloucester. It was to provide a through route serving Newport, Cardiff, Neath, Swansea, Carmarthen and on to Fishguard, with a branch to Pembroke. In the event, Fishguard was not reached until many years later, and this through the efforts of three independent undertakings, later absorbed by the GWR. The South Wales had abandoned its projected terminals at Fishguard and Pembroke, the last mentioned being first served by an independent railway, the Pembroke & Tenby, opened in 1863 between these two points and later extended to Whitland to connect with the GWR.

The South Wales Railway, which reached Swansea in 1850, Carmarthen in 1852, and Haverfordwest in 1854, was constructed to Brunel's 7 ft gauge, and was worked from the start, so far as locomotive and rolling stock were concerned, by the GWR, by whom the line was taken over entirely in 1863.

The engine here depicted, **Antiquary**, is one of a class known to have worked on the South Wales Railway. It was one of a series of ten built by R. Stephenson & Company in 1855. All were broken up by 1876. They were of particular interest in that they were the only 4–4–0 tender engines ever to have run on the broad gauge, which was abandoned on this part of the system in 1872, twenty years before its final demise in England.

Fishguard Harbour about 1908. It had been opened two years previously, when the service of ships to Rosslare, providing a direct route to Southern Ireland, was inaugurated. The locomotive is a small saddle tank built by Messrs Manning Wardle & Company in 1889, named **Hook Norton** and purchased by the Fishguard & Rosslare Railways and Harbour Company (which owned the last mile into Fishguard) in 1907, later becoming GWR No 1337.

The direct route between Clarbeston Road and Fishguard was opened in 1906 concurrently with the inauguration of the new steamship service. In more recent years a service of motor trains was operated between these points and some halts constructed, amongst which were the rather quaintly named Wolfs Castle (1913) and Welsh Hook (1924). This local service, however, ceased in 1964. The original route to Fishguard was via Rosebush, long since closed.

A number of other lines, originally independent concerns, gradually became absorbed by the GWR system. Older even than the GWR itself was the Llanelly, again referred to on page 82, the first section of which, dating back to 1833, was initially worked by horse traction. It reached Llandilo in 1857 and Llandovery in 1858, the last section being jointly owned with the LNWR under the title of Vale of Towy, which lasted until nationalisation in 1948. The extension to Swansea and the branch to Carmarthen eventually became part of the LNWR system (see page 82).

This illustration shows an old long-boiler engine **Victor**, built by Fossick & Hackworth in 1864, and worked until 1881. It was preserved at Swindon until 1889, when it was broken up.

The Monmouthshire Railway was also of ancient origin, having evolved from the Monmouthshire Railway & Canal Company dating back to the eighteenth century, a network of canals and tramroads. It became a fully fledged railway between 1852 and 1855, embracing two principal main lines, between Newport and Blaenavon, and between Newport and Nantyglo, with an important branch to Ebbw Vale as well as sundry smaller ones. This picture is a modern view of Aberbeeg, where the Ebbw Vale branch diverges to the left, the main line to Blaina straight ahead.

Early Monmouthshire Railway & Canal Co 0–6–0ST No 50 built by Dübs & Co in 1875 and later rebuilt as an 0–4–4ST and scrapped in 1908.

Former Monmouthshire Railway 4–4–0T No 14, built at the company's own works at Newport in 1870, as GWR 1304. It was scrapped in 1905.

Associated with the Monmouthshire Railway was the Newport Abergavenny & Hereford, opened in 1854 between Hereford and a junction with the Monmouthshire near Pontypool.

This old engraving shows an iron bridge over the Wye, near Hereford. The engine appears to be a Dods 0–4–0, supplied by a Mr Thomas Brassey for the LNWR, which worked the line for a short time after its inception. The NA & HR was amalgamated into the West Midland in 1860, which was in turn absorbed by the GWR in 1863.

In 1857 the Newport Abergavenny & Hereford, which had already reached Llanhilleth, was extended westwards from Crumlin Junction to Tredegar Junction (later Pontllanfraith) and to Quakers Yard in 1858. This involved the construction of the magnificent Crumlin Viaduct, 200 ft high, length 1,588 ft, over the Ebbw Valley. It was regrettably demolished in 1966 after the closure of the line, although it had been intended that it should be preserved as a national monument. The old woodcut above gives a good idea of this fine structure. Most of the South Wales lines naturally follow the valleys as far as possible; these for the most part take an approximately north to south direction, but the few railways across country travelling from east to west, largely against the 'grain' of the contours, have inevitably to overcome the natural obstacles by means of tunnels and viaducts. There are a number of others, such as Walnut Tree Viaduct, illustrated on page 58, and this, together with Crumlin, the largest of them all, may be taken as representative of several more which it is not practicable to illustrate.

An unusual view of the Crumlin Viaduct showing the workers' gangway below the main rail level.

Another view of Crumlin Viaduct taken in 1963, showing a coal train headed by 0–6–2T No 6627, banked in the rear by 6634 of the same class.

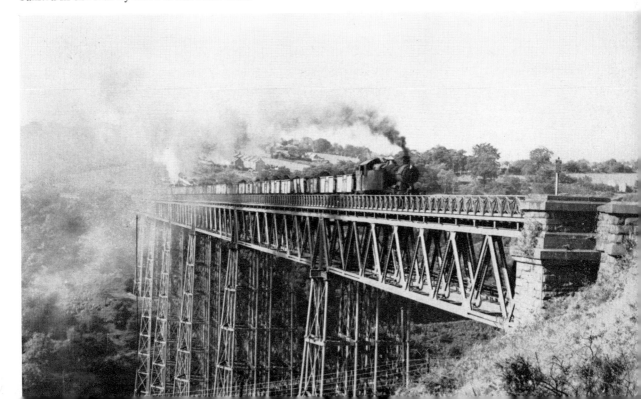

A through train to Neath about to leave Pontypool Road in 1962. The engine, No 6661, is one of a class of 200 built by the Great Western between 1924 and 1928 to replace the many miscellaneous types inherited from the independent companies in 1922. Although some of them were to be found on other parts of the main GWR system, the majority spent the whole of their working lives in the South Wales valleys. This section of the old NA & HR eventually linked up with the old Vale of Neath line, opened in 1851-3 as a broad-gauge line linking Neath with Merthyr Tydfil and Aberdare. It was amalgamated with the GWR in 1865, and the whole route between Neath and Pontypool Road was in later years worked as one section until the through passenger services were discontinued in 1964.

OTHER GWR LINES BETWEEN MONMOUTHSHIRE AND WEST WALES

Apart from various lines in South Wales built by the GWR itself there were a number of other early independent railways which eventually became part of the Great Western Railway system in the last quarter of the nineteenth century and the opening years of the twentieth. Considerations of space preclude mention of all but a few of them.

The town of Monmouth, famous as the birthplace of Henry V, was the focal point of four pleasant, typical GWR, branch lines running through some delightful scenery, the Wye Valley in particular. This scene shows Monmouth Troy in 1931. All of these lines are now closed and abandoned.

Usk, on the Monmouth–Pontypool Road branch, in 1955, with a GWR rail motor train.

The Golden Valley Railway was a somewhat ill fated venture, owing to the very sparsely populated stretch of countryside which it served, notwithstanding the Elysian Fields picture which its title envisages. It ran between Pontrilas on the Newport Abergavenny & Hereford line, to Hay on the Midland branch from Hereford. It was opened between 1881 and 1889 and closed in 1897-8. Purchased by the GWR in 1899, it was reopened in 1901. Passenger services were again discontinued in 1941, this time for good, but a little freight traffic continued over some sections until the 1950s. It is now entirely abandoned. This view shows a train at Peterchurch about sixty years ago.

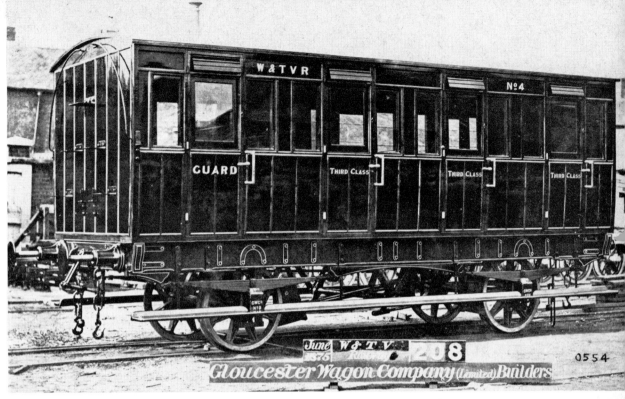

In West Wales there was the Whitland & Cardigan Railway, opened between Whitland and Crymmych Arms in 1873 under the title of Whitland & Taf Vale Railway. It was extended to Cardigan in 1886 and taken over by the GWR in 1890. It was closed in 1964.

This view is an official photograph of the Gloucester Wagon Company, of one of the original coaches.

Crymmych Arms, original terminus of the line, in 1958, with a train leaving for Cardigan.

The Manchester & Milford Railway, conceived in 1860, was one of those grandiose undertakings which never came to fruition, the original conception having been of a through route between Lancashire and Milford Haven, once the principal port in south-west Wales, and long before Fishguard came into existence. All that eventually materialised of the envisaged 207 miles main line was the 27-mile stretch between Strata Florida and Pencader, opened in 1866.

The line between Strata Florida and Aberystwyth, opened in 1867, was an afterthought, and would in effect have been a branch of the M & M if its projected main line, running in a north-easterly direction from Strata Florida to Llanidloes, had ever been completed. (Some earthworks were actually made.)

The line southwards from Pencader to Carmarthen, together with the branch to Llandyssul (later extended to Newcastle Emlyn) was built by another railway, the Carmarthen & Cardigan, there being no legal connection between the two companies. The Manchester & Milford remained independent until 1914, although it had been leased to the GWR from 1906. The through passenger service between Aberystwyth and Carmarthen ceased in 1965, but the southern 35 miles of the route from Port Llanio, together with the Newcastle Emlyn branch, and part of the Aberayron branch, are still open for freight and milk traffic. Manchester & Milford 2–4–0 at Llanylythen in the 1890s. It was built by the LNWR at Crewe in 1855, which railway sold it to the M & M in 1891, on whose line it ran until 1899.

Aberayron branch train at Lampeter about 1913. The engine is 0–4–2T No 559 with pull-and-push coach No 51 and strengthened by two additional four-wheelers.

An interesting survival of the Manchester & Milford Railway, found at Aberystwyth in 1948; an old rail chair in use on the narrow-gauge Vale of Rheidol Railway.

THE GREAT WESTERN IN CENTRAL WALES

The principal sphere of activity, so far as the Great Western is concerned, lay in the southern half of the country. The centre and the north were chiefly the domain of the Cambrian and the London & North Western. The GWR did however have its own independent lines to Dolgelly and Blaenau Festiniog in pregrouping days, together with sundry lines in the Wrexham area. At Dolgelly it made end-on junction with the Cambrian, giving it through access to Barmouth, and the Lleyn Peninsula.

The viaduct at Chirk, on the main Shrewsbury–Chester line. In the background can be seen the well known aqueduct carrying the Shropshire Union Canal.

Berwyn Halt, between Llangollen and Corwen, on the main GWR line between Ruabon and Dolgelly, now entirely closed under the Beeching plan.

1882 saw the completion of the spectacular branch from Bala through the wild and mountainous region to Blaenau Festiniog, where it met with the LNWR and the narrow-gauge Festiniog Railway, both referred to elsewhere. This view is of Bala Junction, one of those curiosities, of which there have been one or two other examples in the British Isles, of a purely interchange station only, without road access, and to or from which one could not obtain a ticket.

A view taken in 1953 near Trawsfynydd on the Bala–Festiniog branch, closed to passengers in 1960. The upper section between Trawsfynydd and Blaenau Festiniog, however, remains open in consequence of the construction of an atomic power station, the waste spoil from which is conveyed by means of a new connection with the LNWR at Blaenau Festiniog away down that line's branch via Llandudno Junction for disposal.

The branch train for Bala Junction photographed in 1953.

THE SEVERN TUNNEL

The estuary of the River Severn from Gloucester, where it broadens out from a mere river into an ever widening expanse of water down to the Bristol Channel, has always been a major obstacle to direct communication between southern England and South Wales. Below Gloucester until 1879 Telford's road bridge was the most southerly means of crossing the estuary other than by ferry. In that year the Severn Bridge was opened to carry the Severn & Wye Railway between the main Midland line and the Forest of Dean. Nevertheless the need for a tunnel or a bridge further downstream to shorten the distance between Bristol and Newport was still a vital necessity. This was appreciated as long ago as 1865 when the idea of a bridge was considered, but it came to nothing. Eventually work on the Severn Tunnel began at Sudbrook in 1873, an immense undertaking completed after almost insuperable difficulties and opened in September 1886 (to passengers in December of that year).

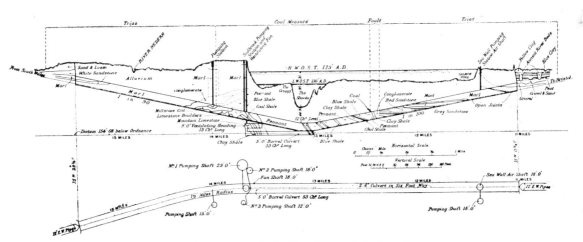

Diagram of the lay-out of the Severn Tunnel, 4 miles 628 yards in length.

From the very nature of the subsoil surrounding the Severn Tunnel, it has always had to maintain a continuous operation of pumping hundreds of thousands of gallons of water daily to prevent flooding. The machinery was still steam operated in 1959 when the two photographs here reproduced were taken, and show some of the dozen or so enormous beam engines required to be in continuous action, together with the coal fired boilers needed to supply the requisite steam. Nowadays the pumping system is electrically operated.

One of the drainage headings below the tunnel itself at its lowest point, the location of which can be seen in the accompanying diagram, shown as a 5 ft barrel culvert, 53 chains long.

The railway provided in later years a regular daily service for the conveyance of cars through the tunnel, between Pilning, on the English side, and Severn Tunnel Junction, in Wales. The train consisted of a single coach for the passengers and as many flat wagons as required for the cars, although the accommodation was limited and it was advisable to book in advance. This shows a train about to leave Pilning in 1959.

View from the passenger coach leaving the exit portal. This facility avoided the long distance detour via Gloucester, but since the opening of the Severn Road Bridge in 1966 it became redundant, and has now been discontinued.

The Severn & Wye Railway bridge previously referred to was a fine structure consisting of twenty spans, 70 ft above water level and a total length, inclusive of the approaches of thirteen stone arches, of 4,162 ft. Although only single track, it formed an important rail link between Gloucestershire and Monmouthshire, being particularly useful as a diversionary route when repairs to the Severn Tunnel necessitated complete engineers' occupation. The bridge itself is situated entirely in Gloucestershire, as rather unusually, the river does not here form the county boundary.

Unfortunately the bridge suffered severe damage from collision by a ship in 1960, and was never repaired. Its final demolition took place in 1969.

THE CAMBRIAN RAILWAYS

The Cambrian Railways, incorporated in 1864, was unique in always being known by the plural in its title, and was by far the largest railway from the mileage point of view of those absorbed by the Great Western at the grouping. It was moreover entirely different in character, being almost of a rural and picturesque nature, whereas the others in South Wales were essentially industrial.

It was the result of an amalgamation of a number of smaller lines, the earliest being the Oswestry & Newtown, and the Llanidloes & Newtown, opened between 1859 and 1861. Eventually it extended from Whitchurch in Shropshire, through the centre of Wales, to Aberystwyth, Aberdovey, Pwllheli, with a long branch (originally the Mid Wales Railway) southwards to Talyllyn Junction, from where it reached Brecon over the Brecon & Merthyr Railway. This latter is now no more, and the few short branch lines have also been closed, but the main system still remains open, although it has been for some time under threat from the Beeching plan.

An old Cambrian 0–4–2 No 7, **Llanerchydol**, built by Sharp Stewart & Company in 1860 for the Llanidloes & Newtown Railway. It worked until 1894 and the photograph, showing the station at Barmouth, must have been taken by that date.

An old view of the original bridge at Barmouth, before reconstruction.

Seen here at Oswestry in 1926 is a Cambrian 0–6–0 of 1919, formerly No 54, as 'Swindonised' by the Great Western after the grouping. This engine came to an untimely end on 4 March 1933 when a cliff fall on the coast line at Friog, below Cader Idris, threw the engine onto the rocks below, smashing it beyond repair and killing the driver and fireman.

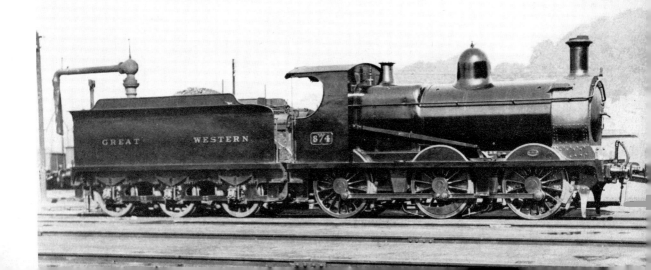

Amongst the smaller lines eventually taken over by the Cambrian was the Mawddy Railway, opened in 1867 and which still retained its independence until 1922, although the Cambrian took over the working in 1911. This 6¾-mile-long branch left the main Cambrian line at Cemmaes Road and ran to the terminus at Dinas Mawddy. Passenger services ceased in 1931 and it closed altogether in 1951. This view shows the train in independent days, with one of the railway's two engines, a standard Manning Wardle saddle tank of 1865. This survived to become Cambrian No 50 and Great Western 824 and was not scrapped until 1940.

Another interesting branch on the Cambrian was that between Abermule and Kerry, opened in 1863. The old picture, at the top of the opposite page, shows one of three engines which worked the line until 1905-7: No 36 **Plasfynnon**, No 37 **Mountaineer** and No 38 **Prometheus**, built in 1863. Passenger services were withdrawn in 1931 and the line closed early in 1956.

The Van Railway was another small branch, by coincidence again 6¾ miles long which the Cambrian maintained and worked for its owners. It ran from Caersws to the Van lead mines. Passengers had been carried only between 1873 and 1879, and it was closed altogether in 1892. It was re-opened however in 1896 under the auspices of the Cambrian, although remaining independent until absorption by the GWR in 1922. It closed finally on 4 November 1940. This view shows one of its two engines, a Manning Wardle 0–4–0ST of 1877, as running after becoming Cambrian No 22.

Afon Wen Junction, an isolated and windswept station between Criccieth and Pwllheli on the north shore of Cardigan Bay, where the Cambrian made contact with the LMS branch from Caernarvon. This latter closed in 1964, with the result that there is now no rail connection between the north and west Wales coastal resorts, save by an impractically long detour via Chester. Afon Wen station was closed at the same time.

It will be noted that there are two water tanks adjacent to one another, that on the left apparently a GWR one and the second one presumably belonging to the LMS. It seems a little odd that one could not have been shared between the two companies, or even why the Great Western needed one at all, being only $4\frac{3}{4}$ miles from its terminus at Pwhelli. LMS trains did of course require watering facilities after their $27\frac{1}{4}$-mile run with a stopping train from Bangor, worked by tank engines. Afon Wen station was actually all GWR property, together with the first 13 chains up to the LMS branch.

The Great Western 'Dukedog' reconstructions of 1936 were much used in later years on the Cambrian lines, and the view above shows No 9005 at Dovey Junction with a train from Barmouth in 1953.

Three Cocks Junction. The Cambrian (formerly Mid Wales Railway) line to Moat Lane on the left, and the Midland line (actually Cambrian property for the first 29 chains) to Hereford straight ahead. Both lines are now entirely closed.

Until 1967 there was a through express between Paddington and Aberystwyth known as the 'Cambrian Coast Express', and this view, taken in 1958, shows the train entering Machynlleth with engine 7828, **Odney Manor**. These lightweight 4–6–0s were specially designed for working over such lines as the Cambrian, which had severe weight restrictions.

A typical Cambrian train at Barmouth Junction in pregrouping days. This 4–4–0 No 21 was built by Messrs Sharp Stewart & Co in 1886, became GWR 1118, and was scrapped in 1930.

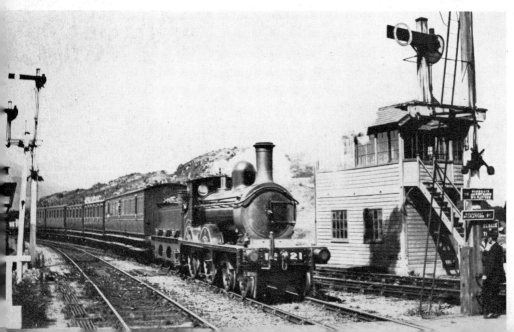

The last through train to Paddington, 4 March 1967, near Breidden, the former 'Cambrian Coast Express' although now shorn of its headboards. The present regular service over this route, which is after all essentially a considerable main line, consists of nothing better than local diesel railcars working only from Shrewsbury. There are still a few seasonal trains between Birmingham or Wolverhampton and Aberystwyth and Pwllheli, and one Saturdays only (summer) through train in each direction to and from Euston, but all without refreshment facilities.

THE TAFF VALE, BARRY AND
RHYMNEY RAILWAYS

We now come to the fifteen miscellaneous companies in South Wales which retained their independence until being absorbed into the Great Western under the Railways Act of 1921, most of them on 1 January 1922, a year earlier than the formation of the other three groups, the LMS, LNE and Southern.

Several of these railways had a good deal in common, in that their very existence arose from the necessity of improving the means of transporting coal from the rich deposits to be found in South Wales. Nevertheless, as might be expected, each had its own individuality, particularly as regards their locomotives. There were over 800 of these, of a wide variety of classes, but with one feature in common; they were nearly all tank engines, as most of the hauls were comparatively short. The Taff Vale, and in earlier years the Rhymney, had a number of tender engines, all 0–6–0s, but otherwise they were very scarce on these lines.

The Taff Vale was not only the largest of the South Wales absorbed lines, it was also the oldest, as already mentioned elsewhere, having established its roots long before the GWR itself had even set foot in the country.

This picture of an early 0–6–0 built by Benjamin Hick & Son in 1846, although of indifferent quality, is included by virtue of its historic interest. It is believed to have been taken in 1849, and if so it is now the earliest known photograph of any locomotive, a distinction which was long thought to have been held by one of a South Eastern engine at the 1851 Exhibition, and more recently by a North British Loco Co official photograph of an engine they built for the Cork Blackrock & Passage Railway of Ireland, in 1850.

With regard to the last named however, more recent evidence reveals that the photograph was more likely to have been taken at Cork after rebuilding in the 1880s.

Royal train on the Taff Vale Railway at Porth in June 1912. The engine, 4–4–2T No 173, was built in 1911. As GWR 1305 it lasted until 1926.

A massive TVR 0–6–2T No 130, of 1916, together with an older saddle tank No 250 dating back to 1867. Both are very typical of many of the South Wales engines, the 0–6–0ST in particular was a type which was much favoured on most of the railways. The 0–6–2T type was also very popular, particularly for passenger work, a standard design being evolved by the GWR after the grouping to replace many of the older engines (see page 30).

The Barry Railway unusually possessed four 0–8–0 tender engines. They were actually built for a foreign railway by Messrs Sharp Stewart & Co in 1887-8, but the Barry acquired two of them in 1889 and two more in 1897. They were incidentally the first 0–8–0 tender engines to be used in this country. Note also the four-wheeled tender.

Train in Barry station in pregrouping days with 2–4–2T No 98.

A former Rhymney engine No 93, shown here as GWR No 136, and very much 'Swindonised'. The Great Western rebuilt a number of the best of the absorbed engines—notably those of the Taff Vale and Rhymney Railways—with typical GWR features, such as in this case their standard type of pannier tank. Others received the well known Swindon taper boilers and lasted for a number of years, many into the 1950s.

The Rhymney Railway had fine and commodious repair shops at Caerphilly, which the GWR and BR maintained as a subsidiary to Swindon and Wolverhampton up to as late as 1964, and it was capable of dealing with a large proportion of major repairs to the South Wales locomotives.

After the grouping many of the older and less standard of the absorbed engines were soon disposed of by the Great Western, and this view shows a line of them in Swindon scrapyard in 1927, the nearest being a Barry 0-4-4T which had been their No 68, but which became No 4 in the GWR list.

THE BRECON LINES AND OTHERS

The Brecon & Merthyr and the Neath & Brecon may conveniently be taken together as they had a good deal in common. Both were essentially industrial at their southern ends at Newport and Neath respectively and both, in contrast to the other valley lines, left the coalfields and ascended the invigorating wide open spaces of the Brecon Beacons and finished up in the county town itself. With a route length of 47 miles, the main line of the Brecon & Merthyr was the longest of all the absorbed lines in South Wales although its continuity was broken in the middle by having to traverse a $2\frac{3}{4}$ mile stretch of line belonging to the Rhymney Railway, and its lower access into Newport was over the GWR.

A pregrouping view of a train on the upper regions of the Brecon & Merthyr, with 2–4–0T No 9. In spite of its lengthy main line, the B & M used nothing but tank engines from the 1880s onwards, although it had had some tender types in early years.

The lonely station at Dowlais Top, near where the summit of the line is reached, 1,314 ft above sea level. LMS type 2–6–0 No 46518 with a Newport to Brecon train in 1957.

Between Pant and Brecon the scenery is of a rather different nature, a magnificent mixture of mountain, river and lake, as shown in this small wayside station at Pentir-rhiw. All of this part of the line is now closed completely and indeed very little of the old B & M still survives. Some of the lower sections at the Newport end still carry freight traffic. The county town of Brecon, formerly served by four companies, is now 20 miles from the nearest railway.

A typical B & M saddle tank with brake van. This engine, No 8, built by R. Stephenson & Co in 1884 (Works No 2497), became GWR 2184 on absorption. It was later rebuilt with pannier tank and scrapped in 1933.

A scene on the lower section of the B & M, Maesycymmer in 1958. Crossing the viaduct in the background is a GWR train from Neath to Pontypool Road.

Coal train for Cardiff Docks passing under Walnut Tree Viaduct, Taffs Well, in 1951, with 0–6–2T No 6608. The lines of three former separate railways are shown here. The train is on the tracks of the Cardiff Railway, which at this point runs parallel with those of the Taff Vale, in the near foreground, whilst the viaduct carried the Barry Railway's extension to Caerphilly.

A unique peculiarity of the B & M was that its short branch from Machen to Caerphilly divided at one section over the River Rhymney, one line on either side of the banks, being at one point half a mile apart. The real curiosity however lay in the fact that each arm had in later years a diminutive halt known under different names, Waterloo and Fountain Bridge, with the result that the down timetable alone shows the name of the latter, and Waterloo is found only in that for up trains (to Newport).

The illustration shows a train at the last named. It will be noted that the accommodation and facilities provided are somewhat less than those to be found at its better known namesake in London!

The Neath & Brecon like the Brecon & Merthyr started in the industrial areas and eventually climbed to considerable heights in the increasingly wild country over the Brecon Beacons, and both of them came terminally to the county town. The one station was owned by the Brecon & Merthyr, but it made end-on connection with the Neath & Brecon 7 chains away. It was also used by the trains of the Cambrian and Midland Railways.

The illustration shows an early view of Brecon station looking northwards. The handsome station building-cum-stationmaster's house will be noted.

An old view of Colbren Junction with Neath & Brecon trains on the left, and a Midland train from Swansea on the right. The 0-4-4T would almost certainly be one of four, Nos 1421-1424 (originally 2621-2624) which spent most of their earlier working lives in this area. They were stationed at Brecon,

along with about half a dozen Kirtley double-framed 0–6–0s, and this constituted the total allocation of the Midland's shed division numbered '5' in pregrouping days, notwithstanding that the railway's total locomotive stock of some 3,000 was divided between only 33 areas, numbered 1-33. Area No 6, Swansea, which covered two sheds, a main one at Upper Bank and a subsidiary depot at Gurnos, also had a very small allocation of only 20 engines or so, nearly all 0–6–0Ts. Incidentally the Midland had no depot of its own at Brecon, the engines being housed at the Brecon & Merthyr shed, which also extended its hospitality to two other railways, the Neath & Brecon and the Cambrian.

0–6–0PT No 9664 on a Brecon–Neath train waiting at Devynock, in March 1962, to cross a train in the other direction.

The oldest Neath & Brecon loco to be acquired by the GWR, No 5, built by the Yorkshire Engine Co in 1871. It became Great Western No 1392, and was scrapped in 1926.

Neath & Brecon Junction signal box, the junction being the actual commencement of N & B metals out of Neath Riverside station, used by its passenger trains, but which was actually GWR property. The signals indicate the N & B line diverging left, whilst to the right runs a connection to the GWR Vale of Neath line. The Great Western main line to Swansea is overhead.

The Port Talbot Railway & Docks, to give it its full title, was opened in 1897 and 1898 from the docks of the Cwm Dyffryn valley to serve the coalfields along the route, together with a secondary line to Cefn. It was mainly a mineral line and passenger services ceased as long ago as 1933. This view was taken in 1959 from an empty coal train proceeding towards Maesteg near Bryn, hauled by a GWR 2–8–0T.

Amongst the Port Talbot's miscellaneous collection of engines were a couple of 0–8–2Ts built in the USA. Foreign importations were very unusual in this country before World War II. These two were constructed in 1899 by the Cooke Loco Co of New Jersey. This view shows No 21 as GWR 1379 and rebuilt with Swindon boiler.

Rhondda & Swansea Bay 0–6–0T No 1 at Treherbert in 1924. Built by Messrs Beyer Peacock & Co in 1885, it became GWR 799 at the grouping and was scrapped in 1927.

The Rhondda & Swansea Bay Railway served a somewhat similar purpose to the Port Talbot, but in this case to bring coal down from the Rhondda Valley. It had been opened between 1885 and 1890. It was later extended to reach Swansea. This section, however, lost its very meagre passenger service in 1933, and the view at the top of the opposite page, taken in 1958, shows the old derelict terminus at Swansea Riverside.

The 1960 view near Cymmner Afan, at the bottom of the opposite page, shows in the foreground the old Rhondda & Swansea Bay line to Treherbert. On the right, 0–6–0PT No 8740 trundles a train down the GWR Abergwynfi branch. This part of the R & SBR line is now disused and trains diverted to the GWR by means of a new connection at Blaengwynfi.

CARDIFF AND THE REST

Cardiff, capital city of Wales, and at one time the world's largest coal port. The Queen Alexandra docks opened by King Edward VII on 13 July 1907 also made it the largest port (at that time) in the United Kingdom for general imports and exports, including cattle. Railway communications were furnished by the Great Western, Taff Vale, Barry, Rhymney, London & North Western Railways, and last, but not least, by the Cardiff Railway, a comparatively new company, promoted by the Bute Docks Co in 1897, and which owned much of the railway system in the dock area. The Cardiff Railway's main line was constructed in 1911 to join with the Taff Vale near Treforest.

Cardiff Railway No 36, formerly LNWR 1181, built at Crewe in 1879 as a 2–4–0T. Allocated GWR No 1327, but withdrawn in May 1922.

Alexandra Docks No 30 as GWR 191, built by Andrew Barclay in 1908 and scrapped in 1934.

Workman's train on the South Wales Mineral Railway at South Pit Halt in 1958. 0–6–0PT No 9617.

It is still possible occasionally to run across one of the old cast iron notice boards of the pregrouping railways, although nowadays they are getting scarce. This rather rare specimen of the South Wales Mineral Railway was found not so long ago still in situ at Cymmer.

Train on the Burry Port & Gwendraeth Valley Railway in pregrouping days. The engine No 2, **Ponty-berem**, was built in 1900, was sold to the Mountain Ash Colliery in 1914 and was at work at least until 1962.

One of the special low loading coaches built by the GWR for use on the BP & GVR. Passenger services were discontinued in 1953.

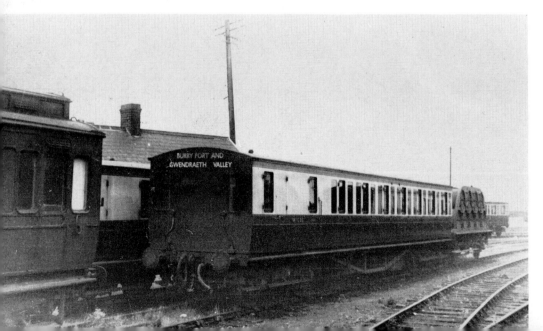

An entirely separate and small concern was the Gwendraeth Valley Railway, with only two engines. One of them still survives in a shed at the Kidwell Tinplate Works, although it has not worked since 1941. This view shows the number plate of the engine, which is named **Margaret**.

Llanelly & Mynydd Mawr engine **Hilda**, which was built by Hudswell Clark in 1917 and scrapped in 1954.

Swansea Harbour Trust train in Swansea Docks. The engines were taken over by the GWR in July 1923, but this Peckett saddle tank, R No 6, had been sold in 1914 to the Cannock and Rugeley Colliery, Staffordshire, where it worked until at least the late 1950s.

A late acquisition to the stud of engines used for shunting in Swansea Docks was made in 1948 when British Railways acquired from the Ystalyfera tinworks the Peckett saddle tank built in 1900 shown, in the picture at the top of the opposite page, at Danygraig in 1948. It attained the distinction of becoming BR No 1 in the Great Western number block, although never actually a GWR engine. It was scrapped in 1954.

Messrs Powlesland & Mason, another concern with lines in the Swansea Docks, also had a number of locomotives which were taken over by the GWR in 1924. This one, No 5, became GWR 795, was sold in 1929 to the Pontadawe Tinplate Works, where it received the name **Dorothy**. Seen below at their works in 1958.

THE NARROW-GAUGE PASSENGER RAILWAYS

Because of the hilly nature of the country, the narrow-gauge railway, after its introduction in the 1860s, was found to be ideally suited to the particular conditions, and many were built, some of which are still in operation to-day. The earliest of them owed their existence to the extensive slate quarrying industry in North Wales, chief amongst which were the Festiniog, Talyllyn, and Corris, all of which were also passenger carrying lines, in addition to the large amount of slate traffic. Others, which remained purely industrial concerns, are dealt with in a later chapter.

It was observed in the Introduction that Wales could claim two distinct pioneerships in railway history, having seen the first steam locomotive to run on rails and the oldest public passenger railway. It might well in addition, in a far more modern context, claim a third such distinction, in that it saw the sowing of the seeds of the modern preservation movement, which has gradually grown during the last twenty years to the proportions it has attained today, not only in this country, but in many other parts of the world. When the Talyllyn Railway was threatened with closure in 1950 its fate seemed to be sealed, but a preservation society was formed to keep it running as a working museum piece, a project which, as is well known, met with success to an extent which even its promoters hardly envisaged, with the result that it was followed by the neighbouring Festiniog. As a result of these two pioneering efforts many other similar societies have been promoted, some of which have also been successfully brought into operation.

Talyllyn Railway **Dolgoch** at Abergynolwyn in 1932 whilst the railway was still in normal operation, without any thought of closure let alone any question of preservation.

Festiniog Railway No 5 **Welsh Pony** as rebuilt, an 0–4–0ST with tender, at Blaenau Festiniog in 1932.

One of the Festiniog double-ended Fairlies introduced in 1869 working a train in the 1920s.

What was eventually the Welsh Highland Railway started life in 1877 as the North Wales Narrow Gauge Railway, but it was not until 1922 that the line was completed throughout from Dinas Junction, on the LNWR Caernarvon–Afon Wen branch, through to Portmadoc, where it joined up with the Festiniog Railway. This view shows a single-boilered Fairlie engine, **Moel Tryfan**, at Dinas Junction in 1925. Latterly the Festiniog Railway worked some of the trains between Beddgelert and Portmadoc. Passenger service ceased in 1936 and the line was closed altogether in 1937, the track being subsequently taken up.

During the last few years efforts have been made towards restoring part of the line, but so far without success.

The 2 ft 6 in-gauge Welshpool & Llanfair Railway, although opened in 1903 as an independent concern, was worked from the start by the Cambrian, and thus absorbed by the GWR at the 1923 grouping.

Unlike the other narrow-gauge railways it had no slate or mineral traffic, its freight being agricultural. The 9-mile-long railway ran between Welshpool on the Cambrian main line, and the small township of Llanfair Caereinion. Passenger services ceased in 1931, and the line closed in 1956. The upper part of the line was reopened in 1963 under the efforts of a preservation society, but no longer runs into Welshpool. Formerly it ran through the streets to the GWR station, and this view shows one of the two engines, No 822 **The Earl**, at this location in 1948. This part of the line is unlikely to be reopened, as the local council are not prepared to allow the trains to run again along the roads through the town itself. The two engines, **The Earl** and No 823 **Countess** (GWR numbers) were stored at Oswestry Works after closure until the line was reopened.

The 2 ft 3 in Corris Railway running from Machynlleth to Aberllefeni, started life as a horse-worked tramway in 1858. It was not until 1879 that locomotives were introduced, passenger working having been inaugurated the previous year. This view (above) shows No 2 at the upper terminus in 1900. A similar engine, No 3, still survives on the Talyllyn Railway, as well as a much later locomotive, No 4, built in 1921.

The line was taken over by the GWR in 1930, and passenger services ceased the following year. The declining amount of slate traffic made the eventual closing of the line inevitable, but the end came suddenly in August 1948 when severe flooding almost breached the embankment as shown in the illustration at the top of the opposite page. There was at one time a proposal to link up with the Talyllyn at Abergynolwyn, an ambitious project in view of the terrain, and it is not surprising that it never came to anything.

After the closure of the Corris Railway, the two surviving engines were acquired by the neighbouring Talyllyn line, then just getting under way as the first preserved railway under private enterprise.

This view shows No 4, built by Kerr Stuart, as recently running with a Giesl ejector. Whilst the chimney is not exactly an aesthetic improvement, it was nevertheless to result in a worthwhile economy in coal consumption. It is interesting to note that the two engines, Nos 3 and 4, carried the same numbers under four successive ownerships, the Corris, Great Western (which took over the line in 1930), British Railways and Talyllyn.

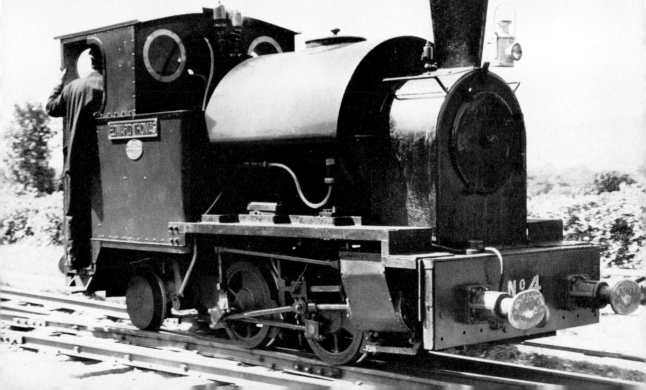

The Snowdon Mountain is Britain's only rack railway, although a number are to be found in Europe, particularly in Switzerland. It was opened in 1896. At first there were five engines, but No 1 had a very short life indeed, being blown down a ravine after only a few months. Nos 2 to 5 are however still at work, together with a later design, Nos 6 to 8, built in 1922-3. This view, taken in 1926, shows No 6 **Padarn** at the passing loop at Clogwyn, with a descending train in the distance. The signalling system has now been abandoned. The summit, 3,540 ft above sea level is, as might be expected, the highest rail altitude in the British Isles.

A recent view, showing one of the earlier engines, No 4 **Snowdon**. It will be noticed that the coaches now have enclosed sides. Trains are prohibited from running on the top section when the wind exceeds a certain gale force.

The ABT system is used, which involves twin-toothed rails in the centre of the track between the running rails, the gauge of which is 2 ft 7½ in. The engines are of the 0–4–2T type, with a pair of cog-wheel axles, worked by separate cylinders situated above the coupled rail-running wheels. The two units of Walschaerts valve gear operate all four cylinders. The boilers are set at such an angle that the water maintains an even level and covers the firebox when the engine is on the normal gradient of 1 in 5.5.

There are three passing loops, at Hebron, Halfway and Clogwyn, to allow for a continuous service at half-hourly intervals during the height of the summer season, the journey taking an hour in each direction.

A year before the W & LR, the 1 ft 11½ in-gauge Vale of Rheidol had been opened in 1902 from Aberystwyth to Devil's Bridge, an exceedingly picturesque route. This also was later acquired by the Cambrian in 1913, passing in turn to the GWR and to BR in 1948. A passenger service still operates during the summer months, and the line now possesses the unique distinction of being the only section of British Railways still steam worked. 2–4–0T No 3 **Rheidol**, built by Bagnall's in 1901, was used in the construction of the line and later used in ordinary service, as seen in the illustration. The present locomotive stock consists of three 2–6–2Ts, one of them built in 1902, a sister engine having been scrapped in 1932. Two other engines to the same design were constructed by the GWR at Swindon in 1923, when **Rheidol** was withdrawn. A recent view of the Vale of Rheidol appears as the last illustration in the book.

The Fairbourne Railway, on the west coast of Merioneth, is rather more than a mere miniature pleasure railway. This $1\frac{1}{2}$-mile-long line serves a useful need as it gives Fairbourne a direct link with Barmouth by means of a ferry which runs from its outer terminus at Penrhyn Point. It was originally a 2 ft-gauge horse tramway, dating back to 1890, but was converted in 1916 by Narrow Gauge Tramways Limited, associated with the well known model-making firm of Bassett Lowke, who built the Atlantic engine **Count Louis**, shown in the photograph which was taken in 1956. The present gauge is 1 ft 3 in.

Several interesting locomotives have worked on the railway, one of the first of which was a small 0–4–0T which had originated on Sir Arthur Heywood's miniature railway at Duffield Bank, Derbyshire, and which had certain features embodying ideas used by Charles Spooner, of Festiniog fame. This engine **Katie** was however worn out and not much used on the Fairbourne. Another interesting engine was based on the design of a Great Northern Stirling 8 ft single-wheeler, but inevitably could only be used with a light load of about two coaches. She was sold in 1939. Latterly a number of diesels have been introduced, but as recently as 1963 a new steam locomotive was obtained, in some ways the most interesting of all, being a 2–4–2 tender engine, a type hitherto almost unknown in this country, named **Sian**.

PASSENGER TRAMWAYS

Purely urban tramways, the benefit of which was once enjoyed by practically all the principal towns and cities in the country, and including of course Cardiff, Newport and Swansea, hardly come within the category of railways in its widest sense. No history of the Welsh railways would however be complete without reference to the Swansea & Mumbles Railway, already mentioned in page 8, which started life in 1807 as the Oystermouth Railway, operated of course by horses (see illustration on page 8) and what could rightfully claim to be the oldest public passenger railway in the world.

The Mumbles Railway in steam days. This phase of the line's history lasted from 1877 to 1925.

Car No 1 of the electrified Mumbles Railway at Swansea Bay in 1951. On the right are the LNWR lines to Victoria station, terminus of the North Western's roundabout route to Swansea, 95½ miles from Craven Arms in Shropshire over the Central Wales line.

This final section was once owned by the ancient Llanelly Railway (like the Mumbles Railway, it is now entirely closed).

In Denbighshire there used to run another roadside tramway between Chirk on the GWR main line to Glynceiriog, a distance of 6½ miles, close to the Welsh border.

Such systems, although at one time common in Belgium, Holland, France and other European countries, were rare in the United Kingdom. (Two other such examples were however the Wisbech & Upwell and the Wantage Tramway, as well as a few in Ireland.)

This view shows the train at Glynceiriog in 1932. This was a 2 ft 4½ in narrow-gauge line.

The Llandudno & Colwyn Bay Tramway might also be described as a small railway operating between these two points, a distance of about 5 miles, much of it on reserved tracks away from public roads. The last tram ran on 24 March 1956.

Also at Llandudno, this time still in operation, is to be found a funicular tramway, unique in these islands, which climbs the Great Orme to a height of 679 ft. It is worked in two sections, passengers change cars at the half way house. Built in 1902, it is cable worked by two winding engines at the central winding house. Until October 1957 the power was supplied by colliery-type steam winding engines, one for each section. During the winter months it was converted to electrical operation, which began early in 1958. Cars ascend and descend simultaneously on each section, and are counterbalanced. The gauge is 3 ft 6 in.

This view of a descending car on the lower section, taken in 1953, illustrates well the steepness of the gradient, which varies between 1 in 4 and 1 in 6, by the sharp terracing of the houses.

MISCELLANEOUS RAILWAYS

Three other odd railways of particular interest and worthy of mention, which hardly come into any of the previous categories, may now be given brief attention.

The Saundersfoot Railway in Pembrokeshire was of ancient origin, having been authorised in 1829 and opened in 1832. It was a mineral line, with the unusual gauge of 4 ft $0\frac{3}{8}$ in, built for the conveyance of coal from the local collieries down to the coast at Saundersfoot Harbour, a distance of some 5 miles. It enjoyed a prosperous existence until after World War I, when its fortunes gradually declined, being finally closed in 1939.

What was latterly the Shropshire & Montgomery Railway had the unique distinction of having twice in its chequered career been closed and abandoned and subsequently resuscitated. Its first phase, under the title of Potteries Shrewsbury & North Wales Railway, lasted from 1866 to 1880. A new concern, the Shropshire Railways, reconstructed the line in 1891, but unfortunately financial difficulties prevented it from being actually reopened, and it was once more allowed to fall into dereliction. Nevertheless, in 1907, the Shropshire & Montgomeryshire Railway was formed under the provisions of the Light Railways Act, under the managership of Colonel H. F. Stephens, an ardent promoter of light railways, and reopened in 1911. It continued to serve the modest needs of the district until World War II when it was taken over by the War Department, a large number of ammunition dumps being constructed along the side of the line. It was finally closed in 1960.

The Bishops Castle opened in 1865, ran from Craven Arms, on the Welsh Border, to the small town of its name in Shropshire. Its larger ambitions were never realised, but in spite of perpetual financial difficulties it managed to maintain a precarious existence until 1935.

The Saundersfoot Railway never ran a public passenger service, but regular trains were operated for the benefit of the miners. This 0–4–0ST was built by Manning Wardle & Co Ltd (Works No 476) in 1874. It lasted until the closure of the line in 1939.

Potteries Shrewsbury & North Wales Railway train at Shrewsbury in the 1870s. The engine is an 0–4–2 obtained from the LNWR, built by Bury Curtis & Kennedy in 1847.

The scene of dereliction at Kinnerley about 1902, after the second abandonment of the line.

Kinnerley shed, Shropshire & Montgomeryshire Railway, in 1926. Amongst the miscellaneous collection of locomotives working the railway at the time, under the managership of Colonel Stephens, can be seen the diminutive No 1 **Gazelle** (now preserved at Longmoor, Hants), a LB & SCR Terrier No 8 **Dido**, a LSWR Ilfracombe goods No 6 **Thisbe** and another Brighton No 9 **Daphne**.

S & MR train entering Llanymynech in 1932, where the line made connection with the former Cambrian Railways, with another acquisition, this time an LNWR Webb 0–6–0 No 8102. The somewhat optimistic notice 'Frequent trains to Shrewsbury' could hardly be said to conform with modern ideas of frequency, as there were in fact just six trains a day with, it must be added, two extra on Saturdays!

A train on the Bishops Castle in 1932, during the last few years of its existence. The engine, **Carlisle**, built by Kitson & Co in 1867 (Works No 1421), which had worked most of the traffic since 1895, relieved by a GWR 0–4–2T purchased in 1905. It will be noted that it had acquired certain Swindon characteristics such as the chimney and safety valve cover.

COAL AND OTHER INDUSTRIES

The rich South Wales coalfield is of course a very important factor, not only in the Principality itself, but in the whole economy of Britain, and any account of the railways of Wales, must necessarily include a brief survey of the major part of the development and prosperity of this industry. Welsh coal is noted for its good quality, particularly anthracite, of which the main deposits are at the western end of Glamorgan.

The necessity for conveyance of coal from the valleys down to the ports of Newport, Cardiff, Porthcawl and Llanelly for shipment was the reason for construction of most of the valley lines, of which the Taff Vale, already referred to on pages 52 and 53, was the major pioneer. Some of the others are also dealt with under the individual headings on pages 54-69.

Closely associated with coal mining was of course the iron and steel industry, with its large plants at Ebbw Vale, Merthyr Tydfil, Dowlais, Cardiff, Margam, Port Talbot, Llanelly and other centres.

There are also considerable numbers of tinplate works, principally in West Glamorgan. Copper was at one time an important industry in the western part of the coalfield, particularly in the Swansea area, where copper smelting is still carried on.

A typical South Wales colliery scene, at Celynon, Crumlin.

Aberbargoed, a typical Welsh mining village, showing the Rhymney Railway single branch line over which the Brecon and Merthyr trains from Newport to Brecon ran before passing on to its own metals again at Deri. The slagheap in the background well illustrates the potential danger of these tips in the proximity of the little township, as was well typified by the disastrous Aberfan tragedy of 1966.

Another impressive view of a colliery scene representative of the Welsh valleys, showing the Maritime pit at Pontypridd, in the well known Rhondda Valley, heart of the South Wales coalfield.

The Ebbw Vale Steel Company (now owned by Messrs Richard Thomas & Baldwins Limited) had a line, 8 miles in length, serving its quarries at Trefil, high up in the southern range of the Brecon Mountains, from whence it obtained its supplies of limestone. This is of particular interest in that it attained a summit of 1,600 ft above sea level, and was the highest altitude attained by a standard-gauge railway in the British Isles, well exceeding the 1,484 ft at Druimuachdar on the Highland, well known as being the highest main line railway.

This illustration depicts a private rail tour over the line, which took place on 7 June 1959, the engine being an 0–6–0ST, built by Robert Stephenson & Co in 1937, Works No 4144.

An interesting old engine working at Mountain Ash colliery in 1958, built by Fox Walker in 1874 (Works No 242). It is now preserved at Bristol.

The Garratt type of locomotive has never been used in this country to any extent. The well known Gresley 2–8–8–2 working the Worsboro' incline, and the thirty-three 2–6–6–2s built for the LMS for heavy coal trains were the only main line application of the design, but there were also a few smaller 0–4–4–0 engines built for industrial use. One of these, which appeared in 1924 at Messrs Vivan & Son's works at Hafod, Swansea, was in fact actually the first Garratt in the country. A very similar engine is seen here (opposite above) at Messrs Guest Keen & Baldwins works, Cardiff, in 1951. It had been built by Messrs Beyer Peacock & Co—as were all Garratts—in 1934, and worked until 1959.

Llanelly (now redesignated Llanelli) Steelworks, one of several engines with cut-down boiler mountings for working in the steel furnace. They only emerged from these hot confines out into the open when in need of servicing. They have now been superseded by diesels.

The high mountainous area of Wales is particularly suitable for the construction of water reservoirs to supply the industrial areas, and many natural lakes in these regions have been adapted to serve the needs of mankind.

One such is the Elan Valley in Radnorshire, and a small railway once existed between Rhyader on the Cambrian Railways' branch from Moat Lane, to various sites where work was proceeding. It was in operation from 1894 to 1906.

This interesting photograph shows a Royal Train, on 21 July 1904, when King Edward inspected the opening of a new dam at Craig Goch, built to supply water to Birmingham. The locomotive **Calettwr**, is an 0–6–0ST built by Messrs Manning Wardle & Co in 1895. It was sold in 1906 and was until quite recently at work at Corby Ironstone Quarries, Northants, although the fact that it had the rare distinction of being one of the few industrial engines ever to have achieved the honour of hauling a Royal Train was latterly largely forgotten.

Shipbuilding on a large scale is of course associated with the Clyde, Tyneside, Belfast and other places in the North, and never had a place in the Welsh economy. This photograph, however, shows a small yard which appears to have existed at some time at Sudbrook, Monmouth, near to the entrance to the Severn Tunnel.

THE SLATE QUARRYING INDUSTRY

In the counties of Caernarvon and Merioneth are to be found the greatest deposits of slate in the world, and quarrying has been going on in a large way for at least two centuries, although it is now a dying industry as the demand for slate in the modern world has declined considerably.

In early days it was conveyed locally over primitive tramroads, with horse traction, to a suitable port from which it could be shipped by sea to other parts of Britain and abroad. The coming of the steam age resulted in this new form of transport being applied on a large scale to the existing tramroads and extension of new ones, opening wide new possibilities on a far larger scale than hitherto possible for exploiting this valuable industry.

The Festiniog and Talyllyn Railways and several of the other narrow-gauge passenger lines already dealt with earlier, owed their very existence in the first place to the slate traffic, but we are now concerned with the many purely industrial systems.

One of the oldest quarries was to be found at Bethesda; it was originally owned by Lord Penrhyn. The earliest locomotives employed after the introduction of steam in the 1870s were of the de Winton vertical boiler type, as illustrated on page 102.

From 1882 the Hunslet type of saddle tanks, as illustrated by **Nesta** shown on the bare upper reaches, were built in considerable quantity. Note the double flanged wagon wheels, a peculiarity of many of these quarry systems. Each wheel was also loose on its axle.

One of the lengthy cable operated inclines showing a train of loaded wagons descending. These counter-balanced the ascending empties, not visible in the picture, by means of a cable and winding drum at the summit.

Lord Penrhyn made many improvements to the system, including, in 1801, the construction of a railway 6 miles in length, to the coast, over which the slate trains were worked by horses assisted by gravity for which the gradual descending gradient was favourable. This view is taken from a descending train in steam days, the engine being **Blanche**, now to be found on the Festiniog Railway. The line was reconstructed in 1876 prior to the introduction of steam traction, a gauge of 2 ft being adopted. The viaduct carries the LMSR (old Chester & Holyhead line) near Bangor.

The lower end of the line was at Port Penrhyn, on the Menai Straits, and the LNWR opened a short branch from its main line in 1852 so that slate could now be conveyed by rail to other parts of the country. This view of the port shows the narrow-gauge system, with a swivelling section over the LNWR standard gauge.

Note also the special design of points necessitated by the double flanged wagon wheels already referred to. The accompanying diagram makes the working more apparent.

The main line and the quarry were almost exclusively worked by steam until the abandonment of rail traction in the early 1960s, but diesels had latterly been used to a considerable extent in the quarries themselves.

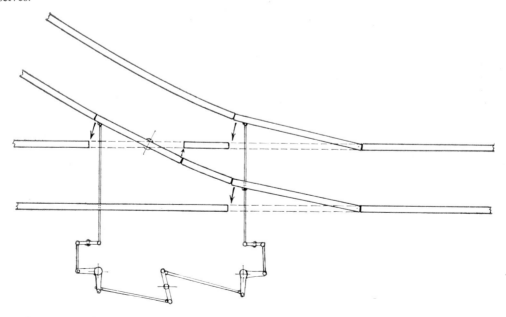

Nearby at Llanberis are the Dinorwic slate quarries, in many respects very similar to the Penrhyn quarries, but on an even grander scale, and believed in fact to be the largest in the world. These two views give a good idea of their immensity, the one looking down giving the impression of a toy model railway system.

Unfortunately the declining demand for natural slate, in these days of man-processed materials for building purposes, gradually made it no longer an economic proposition to work it, at any rate under old methods, and this historic quarry ceased production in 1969. The company was wound up and all its assets sold in December of that year.

This picture well illustrates some of the 'galleries', or 'levels', of which there were no less than seventeen in all, each with its own rail system of anything up to 2 miles in length, and interconnected by double acting inclines, as on the Penrhyn. This mountain of solid slate was actually overshadowed by the neighbouring Snowdon, just across the valley, on which the mountain railway trains could sometimes be seen, or even heard with the wind in the right direction, from the heights of the quarries. Conversely, it was occasionally possible for the connoisseur who knew where to look, to see a wisp of steam over the other side from Snowdon itself, but probably not one in ten thousand visitors there would have been aware, or cared about, the existence of another railway system on the neighbouring mountain. The gauge was 1 ft 10¼ in.

Each level had its own little slate-built shed, and as transporting the engines up and down the inclines was a difficult operation, they tended to spend several years at one location until they had to return to base for heavy repairs.

The top level of all was for a long time the habitat of **Red Damsel** shown here outside its shed, which lonely edifice, nearly 2,000 ft up, was the highest in the British Isles. There were about twenty-five of these engines, mostly built by the Hunslet Engine Company, and similar to those of the Penrhyn. They were graced by most fascinating names, such as, in addition to **Red Damsel**, **King of the Scarlets**, **Lady Madcap**, **Maid Marian**, **Irish Mail**, **Wild Aster**, **Rough Pup**, to mention only a few, and looked very smart in their crimson livery, lined out in yellow and black, very similar to the LMS in its heyday. Many have been preserved, both in this country and in the USA, as most of them lasted until the early 1960s, when rail traction was gradually abandoned.

Like the Penrhyn, the Dinorwic Quarries system had its own main line to the coast, but in this case of different gauge, 4 ft instead of the 1 ft 10¾ in of the quarry lines. This was a separate concern known as the Padarn Railway. The quarry wagons had therefore to be mounted on separate conveying vehicles, as in this picture of a train running along the picturesque shores of Llanberis Lake. At the lower coastal end at Port Dinorwic it was still several hundred feet above sea level, and the wagons had to be unshipped and finish their journey down a steep rope-worked inclined plane. The LNWR constructed a short branch to Port Dinorwic Quay, but the date of building is uncertain. Incidentally, travelling over this line was not exactly the acme of comfort for the occasional passenger enthusiast such as the author. There was no room for a second person in the tiny caboose occupied by the guard, over the bumpy springless journey of some 40 minutes, and there was no alternative to sitting on up ended slates, which produced results best left to the imagination! Still, it was well worth it.

This 'main line'—the Padarn Railway—had been closed in 1963 and the conveyance of the slate transferred to road haulage. However, on the closure of the quarries and the sale of the effects, three of the engines, together with various equipment, were purchased by a private company, to be known as the Llanberis Lakeside Railway, with the intention of re-laying a section of this picturesque part of the lakeside line to the 1 ft 10¾ in gauge, and operating it as a pleasure railway.

The two original engines for the 4 ft-gauge Padarn main line which replaced an earlier 2 ft-gauge horse-worked railway over a different route, were two somewhat extraordinary 0–4–0 engines, **Jenny Lind** and **Fire Queen** built by A. Horlock & Co of Northfleet Ironworks, Kent, in 1848. This is an old view of **Jenny Lind**, scrapped in 1886, but **Fire Queen** is preserved at Llanberis. Unfortunately it is permanently bricked up in a small shed, making it impossible to photograph it satisfactorily.★

There were many other very similar, but smaller, slate quarries in the area, too numerous to mention individually, but which may be represented by the picture of one of the early de Winton vertical boiler engines already referred to: **Chaloner**, at the Pen-y-Orsedd quarries. It has been privately preserved in working order and may now be seen, sometimes in steam, on the Leighton Buzzard Narrow Gauge Railway, Bedfordshire.

Special reference must also be made to the Nantlle Tramway, originally a 3 ft 6 in-gauge line from Caernarvon to Cwm Nantlle, opened in 1828 and worked by horses. It was eventually taken over by the Caernarvonshire Railway (later absorbed by the LNWR) and most of it converted to standard gauge, being used as parts of its line to Afon Wen, the section from Pen-y-Groes to Nantlle becoming a branch. The remainder, from Nantlle to Pen-y-Orsedd, however, remained 3 ft 6 in gauge and continued to be horse worked in 1963, when it was closed by BR.

At the time it was unique on the nationalised railway system by virtue of its unusual gauge and method of operation.

The two views, taken in 1953, show the yard at Nantlle (the rails of the BR standard gauge can be seen on the right), and the Pen-y-Orsedd incline.

* The shed has recently been dismantled and the engine removed to Penrhyn Castle Museum, Bangor.

THE MODERN IMAGE

Finally, to complete the brief picture of the history of Welsh railways, it is necessary to round it off with four views of the present day scene.

Locomotive depot—modern style. Landore shed, Swansea, showing three types of diesel locomotives.

'Merry-go-round' with 32 × 26-ton capacity wagons, Blaenant–Aberthaw, passing cement works. A far cry indeed by comparison with the Oystermouth Railway of 1807!

Oil train of 100-ton tankers near the Gulf Refinery, Waterton, Milford Haven. The engine carries the venerable name of **George Jackson Churchward**, that notable locomotive engineer of the Great Western.

The new and the not-quite-so-new. A recent view at Aberystwyth, showing a diesel locomotive and a train on the narrow-gauge Vale of Rheidol Railway, the engine No 9 **Prince of Wales**, repainted in standard blue livery, and the only remaining steam operated line on British Railways.

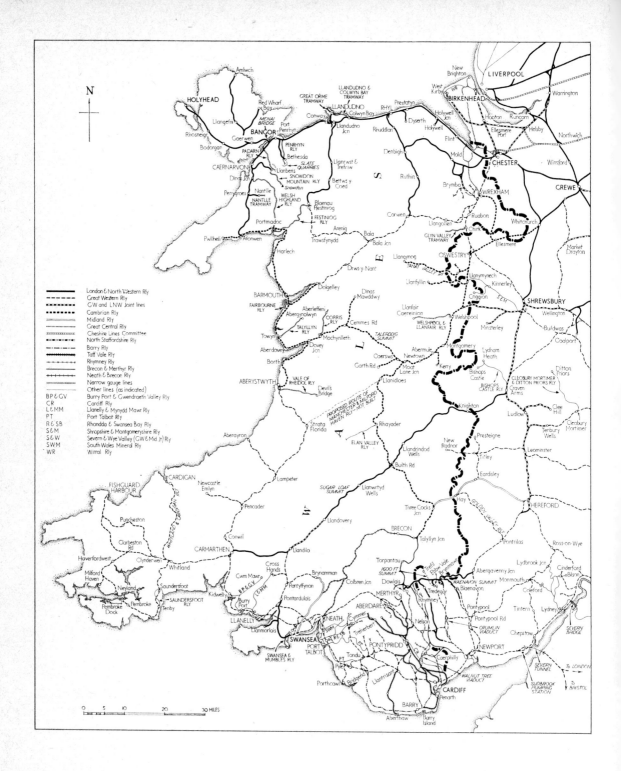

ACKNOWLEDGEMENTS

In a work of this sort many sources of information have to be consulted, too numerous to mention individually.

Amongst those who have assisted in various ways, and to whom I must give special tribute and thanks, are Mr C. R. Clinker whose remarkable knowledge of railway history is well known, and who was kind enough to read through my script and to make several suggestions and also, in one or two cases, corrections in detail of facts in accordance with his meticulous stress on accuracy. My son Mr R. M. Casserley was able to think up several good ideas, and also to supply some of the information in the section devoted to coaching stock, of which he has made a special study.

Special thanks also to Mr T. J. Edgington of BR Publicity, Euston, and to Mr N. W. Sprinks in a similar capacity at Paddington, for supplying several illustrations, as detailed below, together with credits for other photographs where the authorship is known. Remaining illustrations are either from the author's own camera or of unknown origin, this in particular relating to some of the older pictures.

Lastly to my wife for her painstaking translation of my sometimes almost indecipherable handwriting with numerous alterations and afterthoughts, into suitable typescript, without more than an understandable amount of complaints and grumbles.

BR Publicity, Euston: 11 (bottom), 12 (bottom), 13 (top and bottom), 14 (top), 15 (bottom), 16, 103. BR Pubilicity, Paddington: 25, 27, 28, 29 (top), 34, 35 (top), 39, 41, 48, 104, 105, 106, 107. Locomotive Publishing Co: 26 (top), 54 (top), 62 (top), 66 (top), 68 (top), 70, 86 (top), 102 (top). Loco and General Photographs: 47 (top), 74 (top), 85. R. J. Buckley: 49 (top), 62 (bottom), 81. R. M. Casserley: 40 (top), 49 (bottom), 58 (top), 65 (bottom), 71 (top), 93 (bottom), 99. G. Daniels: 56 (bottom), 59, 61. T. J. Edgington: 19 (top), 38 (bottom), 91. W. Leslie Good: 20 (bottom). L. B. Lapper: 50 (top). M. Mensing: 30, 51, 79. W. Potter: 29 (bottom), 58 (bottom).

The painting of the Cambrian Coast Express used as frontispiece and cover picture is by Victor Welch.

INDEX